Contents

A mountain biker............... 2
A mountain bike club........... 4
Bumps......................... 6
Races......................... 8
Under-12s' race............... 10
The track..................... 12
Get ready!.................... 14
Go!........................... 16
Sticks........................ 18
Going really fast............. 20
The run-in.................... 22
Index......................... 24

A mountain biker

My name is Tom and I am a mountain biker.
I am ten years old. I've been riding a mountain bike for three years and I'm in a mountain bike club. I've been in the club for three years.

Every day I check my mountain bike. I check the brakes and the gears. Then I check the wheels. I clean off all the dirt. It's important to look after my bike.

A mountain bike club

I go to the club every day after school. I go there to train. The club coach helps us to train. I'm always learning new things.

The first thing I learned at the club was how to jump on and off my bike. This stops me from falling off and hurting myself.

Bumps

The next thing I learned was how to ride over bumps. It's hard to ride over bumps and not fall off. I have to hold on tightly. A mountain biker needs to have strong arms.

After that I learned to ride in and out of sticks. It took me a long time to learn how to do this. I worked hard at it every day. Now I can ride in and out of sticks really fast.

Races

Our club races every weekend. Sometimes we race at other tracks. Today we are going to race at Boston track. I want to beat my time for my last race. I always try to go a bit faster in every race.

This is Boston track. The club coach helps us to look at the track where we will race. There is a lot of grass on it. It looks like a fast track.

Under-12s' race

I find the place to sign in. I have to sign in to join the race. Today I'm in the Under-12s' race.

Next I check my bike again. I check the wheels, the gears and the brakes. I always check my bike really well before a race.

The track

Then I walk around the track. It's important to walk around the track. It means that I get to know it. I look for flat ground, sticks and bumps. After I've walked around the track, I run around it, too.

I'm almost ready to race. It's time to warm up. I take off my jacket and start to warm up.

Get ready!

I warm up by doing bends and stretches. It's really important to do bends and stretches before a race. It means that I don't hurt myself.

The race is about to start. We all line up at the starting line. I get ready to go. I want to be the first away from the line when the race starts.

Go!

'Go!' shouts the Starter.
We all start to ride fast. I look to my left and to my right.
I don't want to be knocked over.

I put my head down and go as fast as I can. I want to get away from the others. I know there is some flat ground ahead. When I hit the flat ground, I go really fast. Now I'm in the front pack of riders.

Sticks

Next I have to go in and out of some sticks. I am going very fast so it's hard to do. I hold on tightly and don't fall off. I am still OK. I am still in the front pack.

Now the track starts to climb. Climbing is really hard work but I know I must not slow down. If I slow down, I will not keep up with the front pack of riders.

Going really fast

I am over the hill and going down the other side. I am going really fast – too fast to stop. I'm ready to jump off to the left if my wheels start to skid.

I'm back on flat ground again and I'm going really, really fast now. I can see some riders in front of me – but who is behind me? I put my head down and try to ride even faster.

The run-in

It's the run-in. The run-in is the last part of the race. It is flat and straight. I push myself even harder and try to go even faster. I know I'm riding a fast race today. I'm at the finish now.

It's over! The club coach comes over and gives me a drink. He tells me my time. It is five seconds faster than the time for my last race. I'm really happy! I'm getting better all the time.

Index

B

bike 2, 3, 5, 11

brakes 3, 11

bumps 6, 12

C

club 2, 4, 5

club coach 4, 9, 23

G

gears 3, 11

M

mountain biker 2, 6

R

race 8, 9, 10,
11, 13, 14, 15, 22

riders 17, 19, 21

S

sticks 7, 12, 18

T

track 8, 9, 12, 19

W

wheels 3, 11, 20